DISCOVERING AMERICA

Atlantic

DISTRICT OF COLUMBIA • VIRGINIA • WEST VIRGINIA

By
Thomas G. Aylesworth
Virginia L. Aylesworth

CHELSEA HOUSE PUBLISHERS
New York • Philadelphia

C.1

First Printing

1   3   5   7   9   8   6   4   2

Library of Congress Cataloging-in-Publication Data

Aylesworth, Thomas G.
    Atlantic: District of Columbia, Virginia, West Virginia
Thomas G. Aylesworth, Virginia L. Aylesworth.
    p. cm.—(Discovering America)
    Includes bibliographical references (p.) and index.
    ISBN 0-7910-3400-3.
        0-7910-3418-6 (pbk.)
    1. South Atlantic States—Juvenile literature. 2. Middle Atlantic States—Juvenile literature. 3.
Virginia—Juvenile literature. 4. West Virginia—Juvenile literature. 5. Washington (D.C.)—
Juvenile literature. [1. Atlantic States. 2. Virginia. 3. West Virginia. 4. Washington (D.C.)] I.
Aylesworth, Virginia L. II. Title. III. Series: Aylesworth, Thomas G. Discovering America.

F209.3.A94   1995   94-40423
975—dc20   CIP
                                         AC

THE DISTRICT OF COLUMBIA

At a Glance

Flag

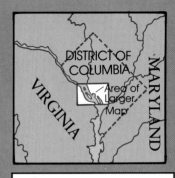

DISTRICT OF COLUMBIA

VIRGINIA

MARYLAND

Area of Larger Map

Flower: American Beauty Rose

Major Industries: Government, printing and publishing

Bird: Wood Thrush

Size: 69 square miles
Population: 588,620

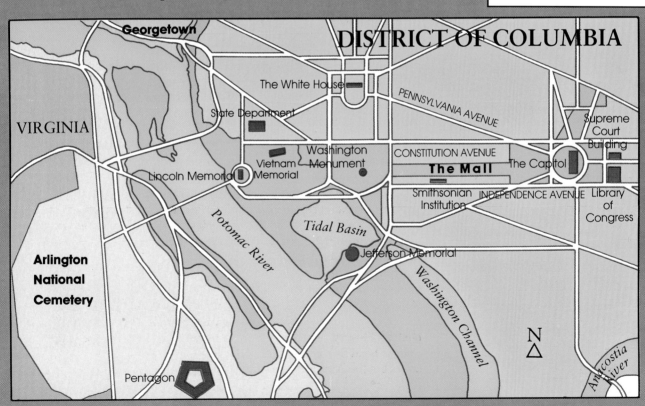

DISTRICT OF COLUMBIA

Georgetown

VIRGINIA

The White House

State Department

PENNSYLVANIA AVENUE

Supreme Court Building

Lincoln Memorial

Vietnam Memorial

Washington Monument

CONSTITUTION AVENUE

The Mall

The Capitol

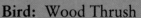

Smithsonian Institution

INDEPENDENCE AVENUE

Library of Congress

Potomac River

Tidal Basin

Jefferson Memorial

Washington Channel

Arlington National Cemetery

Pentagon

Anacostia River

N

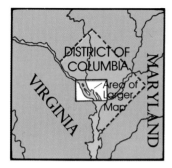

The Mall stretches from Capitol Hill on one end to the Washington Monument at the other, and is flanked by the Smithsonian and many government agencies.

District Flag

The flag of the District of Columbia has two broad red stripes running horizontally on a white background. Above the stripes are three red stars. It is an adaption of the Washington family coat-of-arms.

District Motto

Justitia omnibus
The Latin motto means "Justice for All."

District Name

When it became time to name the federal district in which the capital of the new United States of America would be located, the District of Columbia was chosen. "Columbia," a modification of Christopher Columbus' name, had been a nickname for the country. The city within the district was named for George Washington, the first president of the United States.

District Flower

The official flower of the district is the American beauty rose (family Rosaceae).

District Tree

The scarlet oak, *Quercus borealis*, is the official tree of the district.

District Bird

Hylocichla mustelina, the wood thrush, was named the district bird.

Population

The population of the District of Columbia in 1992 was 588,620. There are 8,531 persons per square mile—all of them in the city of Washington. About 93 percent of the people of the District of Columbia were born in the United States.

Industries

The principal industry in the district is manufacturing. The chief products are printing, dairy and meat products, and soft drinks. Approximately 31 percent of the residents of the District and surrounding areas are employed by the government. And about 33 percent of the residents of the District of Columbia are employed in the service sector—this is the second highest rate in the country.

Government

The mayor of Washington, D.C. is elected by the people, and Congress, along with the city council, supervises district government. The District of Columbia has 3 electoral votes, which it received in 1961. The District also has a single delegate in the United States Congress who was first elected in 1971. However this delegate has the right to vote only in committee, not on the floor of the house.

Sports

Many sporting events on the collegiate and secondary school levels are played all over the District. Georgetown University was the national champion basketball team in 1984, and in 1936, Catholic University won the Orange Bowl football game. On the professional level, the Washington Redskins of the National Football League play in Robert F. Kennedy Stadium. The Bullets of the National Basketball Association and the Capitals of the National Hockey League play at Capital Centre in Landover, Maryland.

Places to Visit

The Capitol. A tour is scheduled for every 15 minutes to tour the Senate Chamber in one wing, the House of Representatives in the other and the great Statuary Hall.

Supreme Court of the United States. Except when the court is in session, tours are conducted every hour.

Library of Congress. This contains some 80 million books, and among the most important are a copy of the Gutenberg Bible and the Giant Bible of Mainz.

The National Archives. Here are exhibited the original Declaration of Independence, the Bill of Rights, and the Constitution.

The FBI (J. Edgar Hoover Building). Tours of the FBI headquarters, featuring exhibits, laboratories, and a firearms demonstration, are conducted daily.

National Gallery of Art. Western European and American art are on display, including the only Leonardo da Vinci painting in America.

Smithsonian Institution. This mammoth complex includes the National Museum of Natural History, the National Museum of American History, the Arts and Industries Building, the

Smithsonian Institution Building, the Arthur M. Sackler Gallery of Asian Art, the National Museum of African Art, the Hirshhorn Museum and Sculpture Garden, the National Air and Space Museum, the National Portrait Gallery, the National Museum of American Art, the Renwick Gallery, the Freer Gallery of Art, the National Zoological Park, and the Anacostia Neighborhood Museum.

Vietnam Veterans Memorial. One of the world's most moving memorials is the V-shaped black granite structure on which are inscribed the names of 58,156 dead or missing Americans of that war.

Bureau of Engraving and Printing. A tour shows paper money being made.

Washington Monument. At 555 feet, this is the tallest masonry structure in the world. An elevator takes the visitor to the observation room.

The White House. The executive mansion tours show the visitor five of the house's more important rooms.

The Vietnam Veterans Memorial was dedicated in 1982 and lists the names of those Americans killed or lost during the war.

Lincoln Memorial. Daniel Chester French's statue of Lincoln looks across a reflecting pool toward the Washington Monument, and the Capitol.

Thomas Jefferson Memorial. This is the national memorial to the president who wrote the Declaration of Independence.

Ford's Theater. The theater in which President Abraham Lincoln was assassinated has been restored and is once again a working theater as well as a museum.

The Old Stone House. This is probably the oldest pre-Revolutionary building in Washington, and was built in 1765.

The Christian Heurich Mansion. Built in 1892, this magnificent five-story, 43-room mansion displays changing exhibits about Washington's history.

National Shrine of the Immaculate Conception. This is the largest Roman Catholic church in the country.

Washington National Cathedral. The Episcopal cathedral which features carillon concerts, contains the graves of Woodrow Wilson, Helen Keller, and many more prominent Americans.

Woodrow Wilson House. President Wilson spent his retirement in this house, built in 1915.

Cedar Hill. The former slave Frederick Douglass, who became one of America's greatest statesmen, lived here from 1877 to his death in 1895.

Events

There are many events and organizations that schedule activities of various kinds in Washington. Here are some of them.

Sports: Harness racing at Rosecroft Raceway.

Arts and Crafts: Festival of American Folklife at the Smithsonian Institution.

Music and Dance: Concerts at the Jefferson Memorial, Musical programs at the Carter Barron Amphitheatre, concerts at the Phillips Collection, concerts of the National Gallery of Art, Dance Exchange, the Washington Ballet, the Washington Opera, the National Symphony, the John F. Kennedy Center for the Performing Arts.

Entertainment: Cherry Blossom Festival, Easter Egg Roll, July 4 Celebration, Friday Evening Parade.

Tours: Georgetown House Tour, Georgetown Garden Tour, Goodwill Industries Embassy Tour, Pageant of Peace, New Year's Eve Celebration.

Theater: Fort Dupont Summer Theatre, Arena Stage, Carter Barron Amphitheatre, the National Theatre, the New Playwrights Theater, the Warner Theater, Ford's Theater.

Tours of historic houses and gardens in Georgetown are conducted throughout the year.

The city of Washington, D.C. was built along the northeastern shore of the Potomac River, which flows into Chesapeake Bay. The river forms the boundary between the District of Columbia on the east and Virginia on the west.

The Land and the Climate

The District of Columbia is bordered on the west by Virginia and on the north, east, and south by Maryland. It is within the Atlantic Coastal Plain, which is part of the lowland region that extends north and south along the Atlantic Ocean. This part of the plain is sometimes called the Tidewater, because tidal water flows up its bays, inlets, and rivers.

The District lies along the Potomac River between Maryland and Virginia. Its humid climate results in temperatures between 32 and 50 degrees Fahrenheit in January and 69 to 87 degrees F. in July. Only five to ten inches of snow fall during the winter because of the District's southerly location.

The White House, on Pennsylvania Avenue, is the official residence of the president of the United States. Construction began in 1792. James Hoban designed the building, whose south portico has often been imitated by other architects.

The Supreme Court building is across the street from the Capitol, next to the Library of Congress. As members of the nation's highest court, the nine justices of the Supreme Court are empowered to interpret the Constitution; their rulings have affected the course of American history.

A view from the Washington Monument of the vast sweep of the Mall, which stretches all the way down to Capitol Hill. The district owes its unusual design to Pierre Charles L'Enfant, a Frenchman who volunteered to fight in the American Revolution and later remodeled New York's old city hall as Federal Hall, where George Washington was inaugurated. Inspired by the French capital of Versailles, L'Enfant spurned the common rectangular grid design in

favor of wide, radiating boulevards, extensive parks, open vistas, and prominent public buildings. From the quaint elegance of Georgetown to the distinctive architecture of the foreign embassies around Sheridan Circle to the natural beauty of the cherry trees in blossom around famous national monuments, Washington, D.C, is still a city with immense character.

At right:
The Jefferson Memorial, south of the Tidal Basin, was dedicated in 1943, on the 200th anniversary of President Jefferson's birth.

Far right:
Cherry trees in blossom along The Mall with the Washington Monument in the distance.

Below and below right:
The Lincoln Memorial, near the Potomac on the western end of Washington's Mall, houses the famous Daniel Chester French statue of America's best-loved president. The 36 columns comprising the monument's exterior represent the states in the Union at the time of Lincoln's death.

The History

The boundaries of the District of Columbia and the city of Washington are the same. When Europeans arrived in what is now Virginia in the 17th century, the Powhatan Indians were living in some 200 scattered villages in the area. During the early 1700s, some Scottish and Irish trappers and farmers built homes on the east side of the Potomac River in what is now Maryland. Across the river, on the Virginia side, plantations were established, including Mount Vernon, the home of George Washington's family. Washington was largely low-lying swampland at the time.

In 1783 the Continental Congress decided that the new nation needed a federal city to serve as the capital of the United States. But the site of the city was problematic, because of the slavery issue. Slave-holding states in the South did not want the Quaker city of Philadelphia to remain the capital because it was abolitionist. Anti-slavery factions in the North did not want the capital to be in the South, since it might appear that the United States condoned slavery.

Alexander Hamilton and Thomas Jefferson worked out a compromise in 1790 by which Northern representatives agreed to set up a new city on the Potomac River. President Washington seemed the ideal person to select the site, since he had lived in the area for years and was also a former surveyor. Washington persuaded local landowners to sell their holdings on the chosen site to the government for about $66 per acre.

The original plans called for a capital exactly 10 miles square on land taken from the states of Maryland and Virginia. In 1791 the purchase of the land from private owners was completed. Washington and an ingenious young French engineer, Major Pierre Charles L'Enfant, set up planning headquarters in a small stone cottage in Georgetown. The city of Washington, named for the president, would be the first planned for a specific purpose.

L'Enfant chose a flat-topped hill, now known as Capitol Hill, as the site of the United States Capitol. L'Enfant's vision was impressive: it called for great avenues, expansive parks, and at least one boulevard a full 400 feet wide. Plans were progressing well, and buildings were on their way up—Washington himself would lay the Capitol cornerstone in 1793. But L'Enfant's enthusiasm for spaciousness ran away with him. He demanded that a wealthy and influential District citizen move out of the path of a planned boulevard—then demolished his new manor house when he refused to comply. Washington was forced to dismiss the young Frenchman, who was replaced by Benjamin Banneker, a distinguished black architect and astronomer, and Andrew Ellicott.

Two years into the War of 1812, British forces invaded Washington and burned every public building except the post office. Plans to protect the capital had proved inadequate, and the city was in ruins until peace came in 1815.

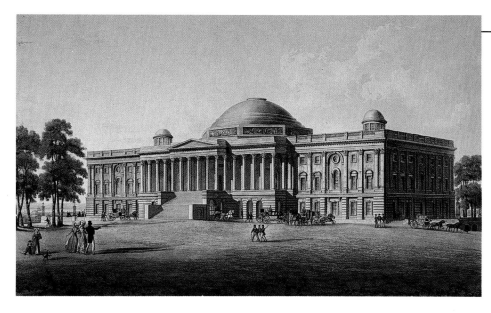

The U.S. Capitol in 1824. Its construction was interrupted repeatedly between 1793, when President George Washington laid the cornerstone, and 1850, when the building was completed.

The basic concept was L'Enfant's, but preserving it has not been easy. For one thing, not all heads of government have shared his reverence for clear-spaced grandeur. Andrew Jackson, for example, is rumored to have planted the great gray Treasury Building directly in the way of a planned White House-Capitol vista with an arbitrary wave of his cane. Another problem was construction stoppages due to chronic lack of funds. Although work on the Capitol began in 1793, the permanent 4,500-ton cast-iron dome was not in place for Lincoln's 1861 inaugural; work on the Washington Monument stood still for 20 years—a fact permanently reflected in its two-toned marble facing.

In the beginning, Congress planned to build the rest of the government buildings on the high plateau east of the Capitol. But when they tried to buy the land, it had been purchased by speculators who were going to charge too much money. So Congress changed its plans and bought the marshy ground west of the Capitol. The north section of the Capitol was completed in 1800, and Congress held its first session in the building in November of that year. President John Adams had moved to Washington from Philadelphia five months earlier.

The City of Washington was incorporated in 1802. (The District of Columbia was created as a municipal corporation in 1871, comprising Washington, Georgetown, and Washington County.) In 1814, during the War of 1812, British forces captured Washington and burned the Capitol, the White House, and other government buildings, but their reconstruction was complete by 1819. Washington's economy and population began growing rapidly, as the demands of government increased. But for many years, District development remained well within its original geographical boundaries. In fact, 50 years after its original purchase, Virginia's land was returned, unused, to its original owners.

The first great expansion of Washington occurred during the Civil War. Confederate forces tried to capture the capital repeatedly, and large Union armies had to be quartered in unsightly temporary buildings. In 1871 Congress approved funds to replace these buildings and to improve the appearance of the city.

William Henry Harrison, the ninth president of the United States, was inaugurated on the steps of the Capitol in 1841. As the city of Washington grew larger and more sophisticated during the 1800s, it assumed its rightful place as a focal point of the nation's intellectual, social, and cultural life.

The capital's second major expansion came during World War I, when carpenters put up what were intended to be temporary buildings along Constitution Avenue to provide office space for additional workers. Some of these buildings still stand. Washington increased in both size and importance again during the Great Depression of the 1930s, when the federal government became the primary agent of relief and recovery. Many new office buildings were constructed for increasing activities, but even these could not hold all the workers who arrived in Washington during World War II. Government had become big business, and Washington's population spilled over into Maryland and Virginia. This expansion continues today.

Pennsylvania Avenue, which connects the White House to the Capitol, was designed as the city's major thoroughfare. In 1865 some 30,000 people thronged the avenue for the funeral procession of Abraham Lincoln.

21

Following World War II, many government workers moved from the nation's capital to the suburbs of Maryland and Virginia. From the time of the Depression through the 1960s, many black people migrated from the South to northern cities such as the District of Columbia, but discrimination was practiced even in the nation's capital. In the 1960s the eloquent Baptist minister Dr. Martin Luther King, Jr., came to the defense of black people throughout the nation. He led a peaceful civil rights march of over 200,000 people on August 28, 1963, from the Washington Monument to the Lincoln Monument. On April 4, 1968, the famed civil rights leader was assassinated in Memphis, Tennessee. Riots broke out in Washington lasting 3 days. Buildings were set on fire; stores were looted; nine people lost their lives; 3,263 people were arrested; and over 11,000 troops were called in to settle the uproar. From the 1970s to the present, the District of Columbia, like many American cities, has continued to suffer from poverty, drug abuse, and the highest crime rate in the country.

In 1963 thousands of Americans took part in the Freedom March on Washington, led by Martin Luther King, Jr. Demonstrators converged on the capital to show their support for racial equality and full civil rights for all Americans.

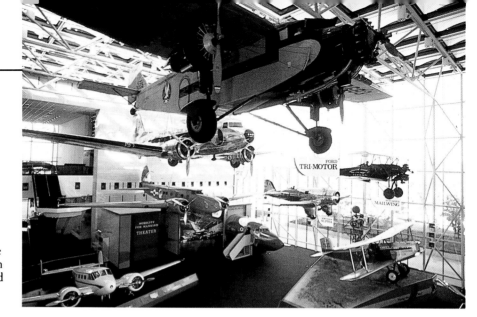

The National Air and Space Museum of the Smithsonian exhibits antique aircraft and scale models of rockets and space vehicles.

Education

In 1804 Congress passed a law establishing Washington's first public elementary school. Georgetown University, founded in 1789, was already in operation. By the turn of the 20th century, there were eight other institutions of higher education in the District of Columbia: George Washington University (1821), Gallaudet College for the deaf (1864), Howard University (1867), Catholic University of America (1887), St. Joseph's Seminary of Washington, D.C. (1888), St. Paul's College (1889), American University (1893), and Trinity College (1897). Washington's Library of Congress is the largest library in the United States, with a collection of more than 35 million items.

The People

More than 93 percent of Washington's citizens were born in the United States, but Washington is truly a cosmopolitan city, with residents representing almost every nation and all 50 states of the Union.

23

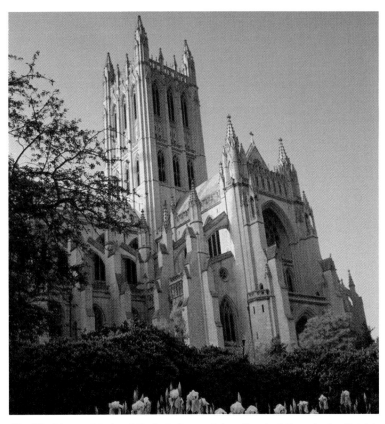

The Washington National Cathedral, one of the tallest buildings in the district, is modeled after English Gothic cathedrals of the 14th century.

In 1846, Englishman James Smithson left his entire fortune to the United States for the establishment of the Smithsonian Institution. This bequest, "for the increase and diffusion of knowledge among men," helped make the nation's capital a center for learning and scientific research.

Famous People

Many famous people were born in Washington. Here are a few:

Edward Albee b.1928. Pulitzer Prize-winning playwright: *A Delicate Balance*

Elgin Baylor b.1934. Basketball player

Carl Bernstein b.1944. Reporter and author: *All the President's Men*

Dave Bing b.1943. Basketball player

Connie Chung b.1946. TV news anchorwoman

Bob Considine 1906-1975.

Early in his career, Edward Albee supported himself with odd jobs such as delivering packages for Western Union.

War correspondent and sportswriter

Charles R. Drew 1904-1950. Organizer of the first blood bank

John Foster Dulles 1888-1959. Secretary of State under Eisenhower

Duke Ellington 1899-1974. Orchestra leader and composer

Marvin Gaye 1939-1987. Soul singer

Goldie Hawn b.1945. Academy Award-winning film actress:

Cactus Flower

Helen Hayes 1900-93. Tony, Emmy, and Academy Award–winning actress: *Anastasia*

J. Edgar Hoover 1895-1972. Director of the FBI

Michael Learned b.1939. Emmy Award-winning actress: *The Waltons*

Anthony McAuliffe 1898-1975. World War II general

Duke Ellington was offered a scholarship to study art at the Pratt Institute as a young man, but chose instead to pursue his love of music.

In l955, New York's Fulton Theatre was renamed the Helen Hayes Theatre in honor of the actress's 50 years on the stage.

Roger Mudd b.1928. TV newsman

John Philip Sousa 1854-1932. Composer of marches and band music

Earle Wheeler 1908-1975. Vietnam War general

Maury Wills b. 1932. Baseball player and manager.

Colleges and Universities
There are several colleges

and universities in Washington. Here are the more prominent, with their dates of founding and enrollments.

American University, 1893, 10,153

Catholic University of America, 1887, 6,464

Gallaudet College, 1864, 2,287

George Washington University, 1821, 16,293

Georgetown University, 1789, 12,084

Howard University, 1867, 11,941

Trinity College, 1897, 1,164

University of the District of Columbia, 1977, 11,578

Where To Get More Information
Washington D.C. Convention and Visitors Association
1575 Eye Street, NW
Suite 250
Washington, DC 20005

Virginia

The great seal of Virginia is circular in shape. In the center is a figure of Virtus, the goddess of virtue, dressed as a warrior. She holds a spear in her right hand, with its point held downward, touching the earth. In her left hand is a sheathed sword pointing upward. Her left foot rests on the chest of the figure of tyranny, who is lying on the ground. Above the figures is the word "Virginia," and under the figures is the state motto. The seal, designed by George Wythe, a signer of the Declaration of Independence, was first adopted in 1776 and modified in 1930.

VIRGINIA
At a Glance

State Bird: Cardinal

Capital: Richmond

State Flag

Major Industries: Textiles, transportation equipment, chemicals, government

Major Crops: Tobacco, soybeans, peanuts, corn

State Flower: Flowering Dogwood

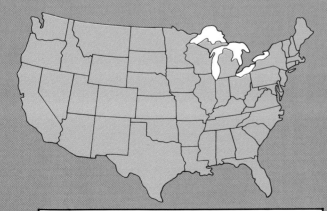

KENTUCKY

JEFFERSON NATIONAL FOREST

TENNESSEE

Size: 40,767 square miles (36th largest)
Population: 6,377,141 (12th largest)

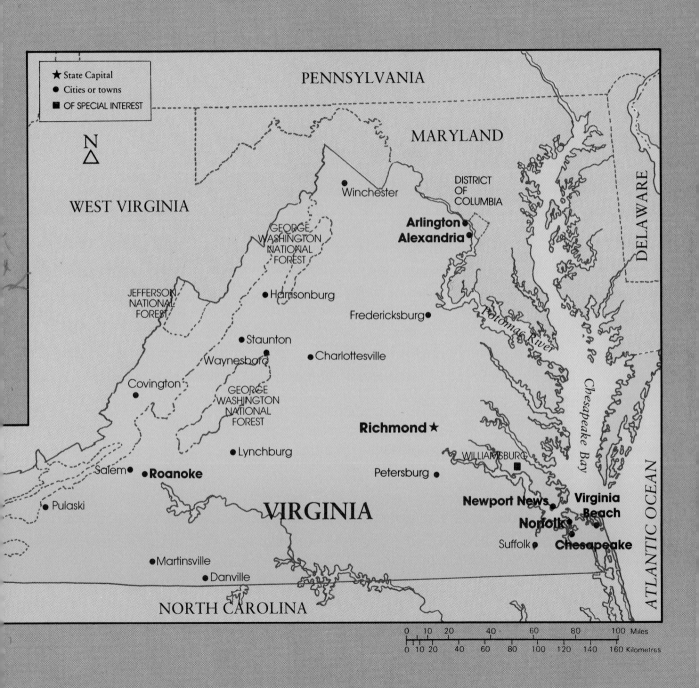

PENNSYLVANIA

MARYLAND

WEST VIRGINIA

DISTRICT
OF
COLUMBIA

DELAWARE

★ State Capital
● Cities or towns
■ OF SPECIAL INTEREST

N
△

● Winchester

Arlington ●
Alexandria ●

GEORGE
WASHINGTON
NATIONAL
FOREST

JEFFERSON
NATIONAL
FOREST

● Harrisonburg

Fredericksburg ●

Potomac River

● Staunton
Waynesboro ●

● Charlottesville

● Covington

GEORGE
WASHINGTON
NATIONAL
FOREST

Chesapeake Bay

Richmond ★

● Lynchburg

WILLIAMSBURG ■

Salem ● **Roanoke**

Petersburg ●

VIRGINIA

● Pulaski

Newport News ●

**Virginia
Beach**

Norfolk ●

Suffolk ● **Chesapeake**

ATLANTIC OCEAN

● Martinsville
● Danville

NORTH CAROLINA

| 0 | 10 | 20 | | 40 | | 60 | | 80 | | 100 Miles |
| 0 | 10 20 | | 40 | 60 | 80 | 100 | 120 | 140 | 160 Kilometres |

State Flag

The flag of Virginia contains the state seal on a field of blue. It was first used in the mid-1800s, but not officially adopted until 1930.

State Motto

Sic Semper Tyrannis

The translation of this motto is "Thus Ever to Tyrants." It dates back to the revolutionary times of 1776, and refers to the colony's desire to break away from the British Crown.

Many pastoral river valleys crisscross the Allegheny and Shenandoah mountains.

State Name and Nicknames

Virginia was named in 1584 to honor Queen Elizabeth I of England, who ruled from 1558 to 1603. One of her most popular nicknames was the "Virgin Queen."

The most common nickname for the state is the *Old Dominion State*, since Charles II of England added the arms of the colony to his shield along with the arms of his other dominions of France, Ireland, and Scotland, making Virginia a true dominion. For the same reason, Virginia is also called the *Ancient Dominion State*. It is also called the *Cavalier State* because the early settlement of the colony was by people who were loyal to the aristocracy of England. Another nickname is the *Mother of States*, because Virginia was the first of them to be colonized. Finally, since so many prominent Virginians were involved in the government of the United States, it is called the *Mother of Presidents* and the *Mother of Statesmen*.

State Capital

The first capital of Virginia was Jamestown from 1607 to 1699. Williamsburg became the capital in 1699. Richmond became the capital in 1780, when Williamsburg was thought to be in danger of capture by the British.

State Flower

Cornus Florida, the American dogwood, was selected as the state flower in 1918. It is also called the flowering dogwood, the boxwood, the white cornel, the Indian arrowwood, and nature's mistake.

State Tree

Cornus Florida is also the state tree, and it was adopted in 1956.

State Bird

In 1950, the cardinal, *Cardinalis cardinalis*, was selected as state bird.

State Beverage

Milk was named the state beverage in 1982.

State Dog

Because of the Virginia tradition of fox hunting, the American foxhound was designated the state dog in 1966.

State Shell

The oyster shell, *Crassoostraea virginica*, was adopted as state shell in 1974.

State Song

The official Commonwealth of Virginia song, "Carry Me Back to Old Virginia," was chosen in 1940. The words and music were by James A. Bland.

Population

The population of Virginia in 1992 was 6,377,141, making it the 12th most populous state. There are 158.7 people per square mile—66 percent of them in cities and towns. About 95 percent of

Virginians were born in the United States, and many are of English, German, or Scotch-Irish ancestry.

Industries

The principal industries of the state are tourism and manufacturing, textiles, transportation equipment, electric and electronic equipment, food products, and chemicals. In 1992 domestic tourists spent $8 billion in Virginia. Many residents are also employed by the Federal Government offices in the state.

Agriculture

The chief crops of the state are tobacco, soybeans, peanuts and corn. Virginia is also a livestock state, and there are estimated to be some 1.73 million cattle, 430,000 hogs and pigs, 157,000 sheep, 1.96 million chickens and geese, and 1.7 million turkeys on its farms. Pine and hardwood timber are harvested, and crushed stone,

Numerous National Parks are found throughout the rolling hills of Virginia.

Jamestown Settlement is a reconstruction of the early Jamestown Colony, complete with replicas of the ships that brought the colonists to Virginia.

attorney general. The state legislature, called the general assembly, which meets annually, consists of a 40-member senate elected to 4-year terms and a 100-member house elected to 2-year terms. These assemblymen are elected from 33 senatorial districts and 63 delegate districts. The most recent state constitution was adopted in 1902. In addition to its two senators, Virginia has 11 representatives in the U.S. House of Representatives. The state has 13 electoral votes.

Sports

There are no professional teams that play in Virginia, but hunting and fishing are popular recreations. Fox hunting is another popular sport in the Tidewater and the Piedmont areas. Several ski slopes have been developed in the mountains in the west.

sand, gravel, and lime are important mineral resources. Commercial fishing earned $90.5 million in 1992.

Government

The governor is elected to a four-year term, as are the lieutenant governor and the

Major Cities

Arlington (population 170,936). Originally, Arlington was a part of the District of Columbia laid out for the capital in 1791. This area across the Potomac River was returned to the state of Virginia in 1846. Today, it is the hub of the urban center of Northern Virginia.

Places to visit in Arlington: Arlington National Cemetery (which includes The Tomb of the Unknown Soldier and the Memorial Amphitheatre), Arlington House, the Iwo Jima Statue, and the Pentagon.

Norfolk (population 261,250). Founded in 1682 when the General Assembly bought 50 acres from Nicholas Wise, a settler, for "ten thousand pounds of tobacco and caske," by 1736, Norfolk was the largest town in Virginia. Norfolk was shelled by the British in 1776 and later burned by the colonists. After the naval

The Iwo Jima Statue at Arlington National Cemetery commemorates the Marines in World War II.

battle between the *Monitor* and the *Merrimack* in nearby Hampton Roads during the Civil War in 1862, the city was seized by the Union Army. Today Norfolk and its sister city, Portsmouth, make up one of the oldest naval facilities in the United States, and are the headquarters for the Atlantic and

Mediterranean Fleets. Norfolk is also a major manufacturing city with fertilizer and farm implement factories and grain and seafood-processing plants.

Places to visit in Norfolk: the Norfolk Botanical Gardens, the Norfolk Naval Base and Norfolk Naval Air Station,

the Chrysler Museum, the Hermitage Foundation Museum, Saint Paul's Episcopal Church (1739), the Moses Myers House (1792), the Willoughby-Baylor House (1794), the General Douglas MacArthur Memorial, the Virginia Zoological Park, and the Norfolk School of Boatbuilding.

Richmond (population 202,798). Settled in 1607, Richmond has always been one of the most important cities in American history. In the beginning, there were skirmishes between the settlers and the local Indians. In 1775, Patrick Henry made his "liberty or death" speech in St. John's Church. The British plundered the city during the Revolution. Richmond became the state capital in 1780 and the capital of the Confederacy in 1861. During the Civil War, it was constantly in danger, and was evacuated in 1865. Much of it was burned at that time. But Richmond came back, and today it is a city that respects the past and the

The Norfolk Naval Base is the home to over a hundred ships, including the U.S.S. Theodore Roosevelt, second-largest warship in the world.

Richmond, on the James River, is second to Norfolk in population but remains the cultural as well as political capital of the state.

future. An educational center, it also turns out tobacco and tobacco products, paper and paper products, chemicals, textiles, printed material, and machinery.

Places to visit in Richmond: the State Capitol, the Governor's Mansion, the City Hall Observation Deck, Monument Avenue, the Virginia Museum of Fine Arts, St. Paul's Church (1843), St. John's Episcopal Church (1741), the Church Hill Restored Area, the Monumental Church (1812), the John Marshall House (1790), Battle Abbey, the Edgar Allan Poe Museum, the Valentine Museum, the White House of the Confederacy, the Richmond Children's Museum, the Science Museum of Virginia, the James River and Kanawha Canal Locks, the Hollywood Cemetery (1847), the Virginia War Memorial, Virginia House, Agecroft Hall, Wilton (1753), and the Meadow Farm Museum.

Places to Visit

The National Park Service maintains 11 areas in the state of Virginia: Shenandoah National Park, Manassas National Battlefield Park, Richmond National Battlefield Park, Petersburg National Battlefield, Booker T. Washington National Monument, George Washington Birthplace National Monument, Fredericksburg and Spotsylvania National Military Park, Assateague Island National Seashore, the Blue Ridge Parkway, Appomattox Court House National Historical Park, and Colonial National Historical Park. There are also two national forests in Virginia— George Washington and Jefferson. The National

Capital Parks Region maintains Arlington House, the Robert E. Lee Memorial, and Prince William Forest Park. In addition, there are 20 state recreation areas.

Alexandria: Walking Tour of Historic Sites. Many historic houses, churches, and shops can be seen while walking through this cosmopolitan little city, founded in 1749.

Ashland: Patrick Henry Home "Scotchtown." This house, built about 1719, was the home of Patrick Henry and also the girlhood home of Dolly Madison.

Blacksburg: Smithfield Plantation. Originally built in 1773, this restored pre-Revolutionary house was the home of three governors.

Charlottesville: Monticello. This is the stately home of Thomas Jefferson, designed by him and built between 1769 and 1809. The University of Virginia. Thomas Jefferson also designed many of the university buildings as well as the vistas, and the serpentine walls.

Covington: Fort Young. This reconstructed fort follows George Washington's original plans.

Fredericksburg: James Monroe Law Office. The future president practiced law here from 1786-1789.

Gloucester: Walter Reed Birthplace. The physician who discovered the cause of yellow fever was born here in 1851.

Hampton: St. John's Church. Built in 1728, it is the home of an Episcopal parish that was founded in 1610.

Hopewell: Merchants Hope Church. The exterior of the church, built in 1657, has been called the most beautiful colonial brickwork in America.

Jamestown: "New Towne." A reconstruction of the settlement of Jamestown as it had expanded by 1620, features original streets and homesites.

Leesburg: Oatlands. Built around 1804, this estate includes a Classical Revival mansion and formal gardens with boxwood hedges.

Lexington: Stonewall Jackson House. This restored home is the only one the Civil War general ever owned, and contains many

Monticello, Thomas Jefferson's home, is the most famous building designed by the third president.

Mount Vernon was the home and plantation of George and Martha Washington, as well as their final resting place.

furnishings that belonged to the Jackson family.

Luray: Luray Caverns. The cave contains huge underground rooms connected by natural corridors.

Lynchburg: Point of Honor (1815). Many duels were fought on the grounds of this restored Federal mansion.

Martinsville: Blue Ridge Farm Museum. This living museum contains buildings dating back to an 1800 farm.

McLean: Claude Moore Colonial Farm. This working farm dates from the 1770s.

Montross: Stratford Hall Plantation. Built in 1725, this was the birthplace of Richard Henry Lee, signer of the Declaration of Independence, Francis Lightfoot Lee, and Robert E. Lee commander of the confederate army.

Mount Vernon: Mount Vernon. George Washington inherited the plantation in 1754, and died here in 1799.

Newport News: The Mariners' Museum. The collection of artifacts that reflects maritime history, including navigation, is housed in 14 galleries.

Orange: Montpelier. This was the home of President James Madison.

Petersburg: Trapezium

Yorktown contains several historic sites, among which is the Yorktown Battlefield with George Washington's original field tent. The Yorktown Visitors Center reproduces a Continental Army encampment.

House. Built in 1817, this eccentric house has no right angles and no parallel sides.

Portsmouth: Historic Homes. The city is famous for its houses dating from the Colonial, Revolutionary War, and Civil War periods.

Roanoke: Virginia Museum of Transportation. This is the largest railroad museum in the Southeast.

Staunton: Woodrow Wilson Birthplace. Now restored, this 1846 Greek Revival mansion is where President Wilson was born.

Virginia Beach: Adam Thoroughgood House. Built between 1636 and 1680, and remodeled in 1745, this may be the oldest brick house in the United States.

Williamsburg: Colonial Williamsburg. Many of the buildings here date back to the early 1700s and many are workshops that are operated by staff in period costume.

Winchester: Washington's Office-Museum. This building was used by George Washington from 1755 to 1756, when he was building Fort Loudoun.

Yorktown: Grace Episcopal

Church. Built in 1697, it was damaged in 1781 and burned in 1814.

Events

There are many events and organizations that schedule activities of various kinds in the State of Virginia. Here are some of them.

Sports: Car racing at Bristol International Raceway (Bristol), Car racing at Thunder Valley Dragway (Bristol), Blue Ridge Horse Show (Galax), Hampton Cup Regatta (Hampton), Virginia Poultry Festival (Harrisonburg), Natural Chimneys Jousting Tournament (Harrisonburg), Virginia Foxhound Show (Leesburg), Morven Park International Equestrian Institute Horse Trials (Leesburg), stock car racing at Martinsville Speedway (Martinsville), Jousting Tournament (Stounton), East Coast Surfing Championship (Virginia Beach), Virginia Saltwater Fishing Tournament (Virginia Beach), Horse Show (Wytheville).

Arts and Crafts: Spring Sampler (Abingdon), Fall Festival (Clifton Forge), Antique Car Show (Fairfax), Plantation Days at Sully (Fairfax), Quilt Show (Fairfax), Market Square Fair (Fredericksburg), Quilt Show (Fredericksburg), Festival of Leaves (Front Royal), Hampton Bay Days (Hampton), Prince George Heritage Fair (Hopewell), Hungry Mother Arts and Crafts Festival (Marion), Highland Maple Festival (Monterey), International Azalea Festival (Norfolk), Pork, Peanut and Pine Festival (Surrey), Boardwalk Art Show (Virginia Beach), Antiques Forum (Williamsburg).

Music: Carter Family Memorial Festival (Bristol), Fairfax Symphony (Fairfax), Old Fiddler's Convention (Galax), Hampton Jazz Festival (Hampton), Blue

Colonial Williamsburg features 173 acres of restored buildings staffed by people in period dress.

Ridge Folklife Festival (Martinsville), Virginia Opera (Norfolk), Virginia Symphony (Norfolk), Richmond Symphony (Richmond), band concerts (Staunton), Wolf Trap Farm for the Performing Arts (Vienna), Virginia Beach Pops (Virginia Beach), Concerts in the Governor's Palace (Williamsburg), Fife and Drum Corps Parade (Williamsburg), Shenandoah Valley Music Festival (Woodstock).

Entertainment: Virginia Highlands Festival (Abingdon), George Washington Birthday Celebrations (Alexandria), Red Cross Waterfront Festival (Alexandria), Battle of Fort Stevens (Alexandria), Virginia Scottish Games (Alexandria), Washington's Review of the Troops (Alexandria), Christmas Walk (Alexandria), Arlington County Fair (Arlington), Dogwood Festival (Charlottesville), Garden Week (Charlottesville), Eastern Decoy Festival (Chincoteague), Pony Penning (Chincoteague), Oyster Festival (Chincoteague), Waterfowl Week (Chincoteague), Danville Harvest Jubilee (Danville), Annual National Auctioneering Contest (Danville), Garden Week (Fredericksburg), Warren County Fair (Front Royal), Middleburg Wine Festival and Vineyard Tour (Front Royal), Galax-Carroll-Grayson County Fair (Galax), Langley Air Force Base Air Show (Hampton), Settlement Celebration (Jamestown), August Court Days (Leesburg), Holiday in Lexington (Lexington), Prince William County Fair (Manassas), Civil War Reenactment (Manassas), Reenactment of the Battle of New Market (New Market), British Isles Festival (Norfolk), Harborfest (Norfolk), Pilgrimage to Cape Henry (Portsmouth), June Jubilee (Richmond), Virginia State Fair (Richmond),

Glassblowing and other crafts are practiced at Colonial Williamsburg the way they were done two centuries ago.

Festival in the Park (Roanoke), Chili Cookoff (Roanoke), Happy Birthday USA (Staunton), Neptune Festival (Virginia Beach), Flying Circus (Warrenton), Fall Foliage Festival (Waynesboro), Washington's Birthday Holidays (Williamsburg), Colonial Weekends (Williamsburg), Publick Times (Williamsburg), Traditional Christmas Activities (Williamsburg), Militia Muster (Williamsburg), Shenandoah Apple Blossom Festival (Winchester), Court Days (Woodstock), Shenandoah County Fair (Woodstock), Yorktown Day (Yorktown).

Tours: House Tours (Alexandria), Christmas Candlelight Tour (Fredericksburg), Warren County Garden Tour (Front Royal), Homes and Gardens Tour (Leesburg), Christmas at Oatlands (Leesburg), Garden Week in Historic Lexington (Lexington), Page County Heritage Festival (Luray), Nostalgiafest (Petersburg), Historic Homes Tour (Portsmouth), Historic Garden Week in Virginia (Richmond), Christmas Open House Tour (Richmond), Historic Garden Week (Williamsburg).

Theater: Barter Theatre (Abingdon), Trail of the Lonesome Pine (Big Stone Gap), Henry Street Playhouse (Lexington), Lime Kiln Arts' Theater at the Kiln (Lexington), Wayside Theatre (Middletown), Virginia Stage Company, Wells Theatre (Norfolk), The Long Way Home (Radford), Mill Mountain Theatre (Roanoke).

Above right:
The Shenandoah River Valley is the largest single valley in Virginia. Its fertile soil and temperate climate are well suited to many types of farming.

Above:
Part of southwestern Virginia lies within the Appalachian Plateau. Rugged terrain, rocky ridges, and narrow gorges form the landscape of this region.

The Land and the Climate

Virginia is bordered on the west by Kentucky and West Virginia; on the north by West Virginia, the District of Columbia, and Maryland; on the east by Maryland and the Atlantic Ocean; and on the south by North Carolina. The state has five main land regions: the Appalachian Plateau, the Appalachian Ridge and Valley Region, the Blue Ridge, the Piedmont, and the Atlantic Coastal Plain.

The Appalachian Plateau consists of a rugged strip in southwestern Virginia with an average elevation of some 2,000 feet above sea level. The area has many streams, some of which have cut deep gorges, and large stands of timber. Coal is mined here.

The Appalachian Ridge and Valley Region extends along most of Virginia's western border. It is a series of parallel mountain ridges with broad valleys between them. The region contains many caves and unusual rock formations that were created by the action of water on limestone. Beef and dairy cattle, sheep, poultry, and fruit are raised here, and gypsum, stone, and clay are quarried.

The Blue Ridge borders the Appalachian Ridge on the east and is part of the larger Appalachian Mountain system. The state's highest point, Mount Rogers, 5,729 feet high, is located here. Tobacco, corn, and fruit are among the region's crops.

The Piedmont is in central Virginia. This is the largest land region in the state, consisting of an elevated plain with low hills. Hay, vegetables, fruit, and corn are grown in the region.

The Atlantic Coastal Plain, about 100 miles wide in Virginia, is adjacent to the Atlantic Ocean on the east. It is part of a larger coastal formation along the eastern United States and is sometimes called the Tidewater because of its many inlets, salt marshes, and swamps. Soybeans, berries, and vegetables grow in this region, and fish, crabs, and oysters come from the coastal waters.

The coastline of Virginia is 112 miles long, but if the small bays and inlets are included, it measures 3,315 miles. The state's major waterways are the Rappahannock, James, York, Potomac, Shenandoah, Roanoke, and New Rivers. The largest lake in the state is Lake Drummond, in the Dismal Swamp.

There are few extremes of temperature in Virginia, with averages running from 32 to 50 degrees Fahrenheit in January and from 69 to 87 degrees F. in July, depending upon proximity to the ocean. Snowfall ranges between 25 and 30 inches in the western mountains, with as little as 5 to 10 inches in the Tidewater area.

Tobacco is Virginia's most valuable crop. The state ranks fourth in the nation in tobacco production.

Virginia Beach, on the state's southeastern coast, is one of the East's most popular summer resorts.

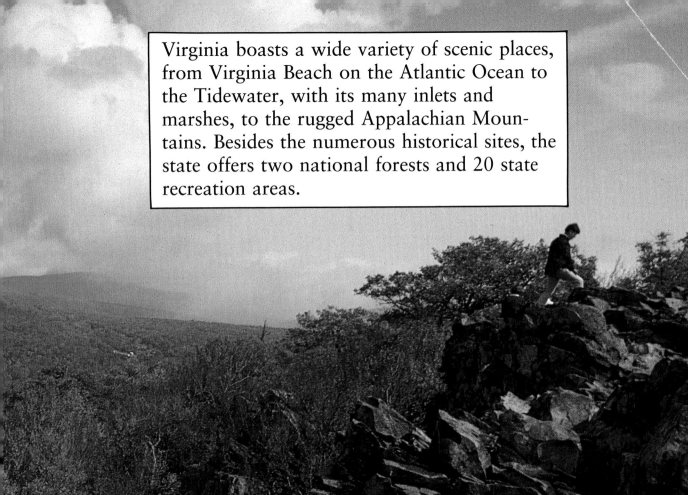

Virginia boasts a wide variety of scenic places, from Virginia Beach on the Atlantic Ocean to the Tidewater, with its many inlets and marshes, to the rugged Appalachian Mountains. Besides the numerous historical sites, the state offers two national forests and 20 state recreation areas.

The History

When European explorers first came to the Virginia territory, Indian tribes living there spoke three different languages. The Powhatan, members of the Algonquian language group, lived along the coast. In the Piedmont region were the Monacan and the Manahoac, who spoke the Siouan language. Other Siouan-speaking tribes lived along the James and Roanoke Rivers. The Iroquoian language family was represented by the Susquehanna, near the upper Chesapeake Bay, and some smaller tribes.

The first European explorers to arrive in what would become Virginia were probably Spanish Jesuit priests who established a short-lived mission on the York River in 1570. Fourteen years later, Sir Walter Raleigh was given a charter by Queen Elizabeth I of England to establish colonies in North America. Raleigh sent some settlers to the New World, but the expeditions failed because of lack of supplies. It was Raleigh who named the area Virginia, for Elizabeth, who was called the Virgin Queen.

On May 14, 1607, settlers from the Virginia Company of London established the first permanent English colony in America on a peninsula along the James River. Members of the settlement, called Jamestown, hoped to reap profits from trade with the Indians. But harsh winter weather, disease, hunger, and Indian attacks almost discouraged the first colonists from staying in Virginia.

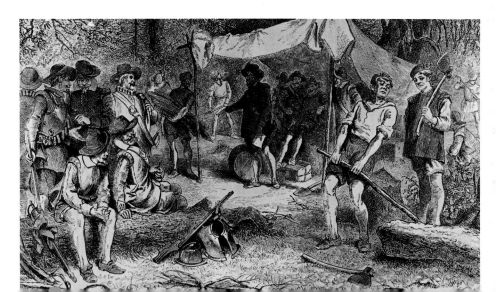

Pocahontas, the daughter of Chief Powhatan, was a child of 10 or 12 when the English settled at Jamestown. Allegedly, she saved the life of colonial leader Captain John Smith when he was captured by the confederation headed by her father. Later, Pocahontas was taken hostage by a band of Englishmen who wanted to exchange her for English prisoners. While she was being detained in Jamestown, colonist John Rolfe fell in love with her and obtained permission from the governor for their marriage, which took place in 1614.

King James I of England set up the Virginia Company of London (sometimes called the London Company) in 1606 to organize the colonization of Virginia. The company sent settlers who established the first permanent English settlement in America at Jamestown in 1607, under the leadership of Captain John Smith. The colonists had a hard life, but managed to survive.

Smith was injured in 1609 and had to return to England. The following winter, lack of food began to take its toll, and many settlers died. But in the spring, English ships arrived with fresh supplies and new colonists.

In 1612 John Rolfe, one of the colonists, began to raise tobacco, which may have saved the colony. Exporting cured tobacco gave the people a new way of supporting themselves. Rolfe married Pocahontas, the daughter of the Indian chief Powhatan, in 1614, and the marriage brought peace between the Indians and the colonists for a time.

By 1619 each settler had land of his own, and the Virginia Company decided to send boatloads of young women as wives for the settlers. That year the House of Burgesses, the first representative legislature in America, was formed in Virginia. Dutch traders brought the first slaves to Jamestown, and Virginians built a plantation economy on slave labor. A landed aristocracy emerged.

Farmers had begun to settle as far west as the edge of the Piedmont by 1650. They resented the fact that the territory was being run by the aristocrats of the Tidewater area. They also resented British laws that limited colonial trade. In 1676 a group of dissenters commanded by the young planter Nathaniel Bacon carried out an armed rebellion. Bacon's Rebellion was the first uprising of its kind in the British colonies. After a series of victories over the repressive governor Sir William Berkeley, and a few minor legislative advances, Bacon suddenly died of malaria. Without its leader, the rebellion collapsed and brought no essential political change to the colony.

In 1699 the capital of Virginia was moved from Jamestown to Williamsburg, and by 1700, English settlers had penetrated west to the mountains. The French, who had claimed the western part of the territory, resented this, and the fourth French and Indian War broke out in 1754. The British defeated the French and their Indian allies, and England controlled the region after 1763.

In the early 1770s, the Indians were attacking settlers who moved into their lands along Virginia's western frontier, which led to Lord Dunmore's War. The conflict was named for the governor of Virginia, John Murray, Earl of Dunmore. Virginia soldiers commanded by Andrew Lewis defeated the Shawnee Indians at Point Pleasant (which is now in West Virginia) in 1774, and the threat of Indian raids decreased.

Virginia's upper class had time for scholarship, for the development and debate of ideas, and for independent thinking. A remarkable group of leaders emerged: the eloquent Patrick Henry, George Washington, the versatile Thomas Jefferson, James Madison, and James Monroe, whose impression on our political philosophy is

George Washington was born in Westmoreland County, in 1732. From this small house on the Potomac, one of America's greatest leaders would emerge.

George Washington distinguished himself early in life as a member of Virginia society. The son of a wealthy planter, young Washington was 16 when he began his career as a land surveyor in the Shenandoah Valley. After gaining a knowledge of the wilderness and experience with the Indians, Washington joined his state's militia. His leadership abilities resulted in a remarkable rise to command during the colonial wars and the American Revolution.

indelible. Virginia would furnish the new United States with four of its first five presidents.

Strong leadership resulted in independent action. In 1774 the British Parliament ordered the port of Boston closed as punishment for the Boston Tea Party. The Virginia House of Burgesses made the day of closing a day of fasting and prayer in support of the Massachusetts colonists. As a result, Governor Dunmore dissolved the House of Burgesses. The members then met without permission

in Williamsburg, calling themselves the First Virginia Convention. They elected delegates to the First Continental Congress.

The Second Virginia Convention was held in March 1775 in Richmond, where Patrick Henry made the famous speech in which he said, "Give me liberty or give me death!" The Second Continental

Virginia-born Patrick Henry was one of the most influential orators and statesmen of the American Revolution. His speeches aroused strong public support for action against the British.

Thomas Jefferson was one of Virginia's exceptionally talented native sons. In addition to writing the Declaration of Independence and serving as the third president of the United States, Jefferson was a respected diplomat, educator, architect, inventor, and gourmet.

On October 19, 1781, after fighting his way onto the peninsula between the York and James Rivers, British lieutenant general Charles Cornwallis was forced to surrender to George Washington at Yorktown. The British force had been cut off by a French fleet, and its defeat effectively ended the Revolutionary War, although the British government did not recognize the new republic until the Treaty of Paris was signed in September 1783.

Congress met later that year and elected George Washington commander in chief of the Continental Army. In 1776 Virginia adopted its first constitution and became an independent commonwealth. Patrick Henry was named governor, and Lord Dunmore was expelled from the colony. The capital was moved from Williamsburg to Richmond in 1780.

During the Revolutionary War, there was a higher percentage of revolutionaries in Virginia than in any other southern colony. Thomas Jefferson wrote the Declaration of Independence in 1776. Virginia contributed the cavalry leader "Light-Horse Harry" Lee and Daniel Morgan, the hero of the battles of Saratoga and Cowpens. Another prominent Virginian, George Rogers Clark, won Revolutionary War victories in the Northwest Territory (roughly the present-day Midwest). In 1781 the final victory of the Revolution was achieved at Yorktown, when Lord Cornwallis surrendered to George Washington.

Virginia ratified the new Constitution of the United States in 1788 and became the tenth state of the Union. In 1792 the westernmost counties of Virginia became the state of Kentucky.

Thomas "Stonewall" Jackson was one of the Confederacy's ablest and most respected military leaders. He won his nickname when his brigade held firmly against the great Union assault at the First Battle of Bull Run, where a fellow officer inspired his men to rally by shouting "There is Jackson standing like a stone wall!"

Robert E. Lee, born in Stratford in 1807, was the South's greatest Civil War general. He commanded Confederate forces from May 1862 until the war ended in 1865. A brilliant strategist, Lee fought in most of the war's major battles, including Fredericksburg, Chancellorsville, Gettysburg, and Appomattox Court House, the scene of his surrender to Union general Ulysses S. Grant.

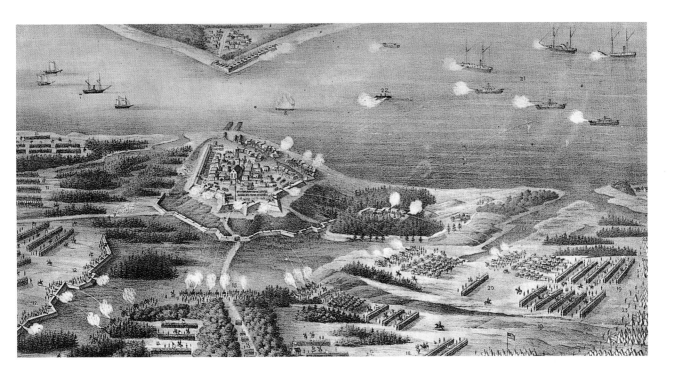

During the Mexican War of 1846 to 1848, Virginia military leaders including Thomas J. Jackson, Joseph E. Johnston, Robert E. Lee, and Winfield Scott distinguished themselves and gained experience that would soon be needed in the Civil War. The paradox of Virginia's history—one of fighters for freedom whose economy depended on slavery—became apparent in 1861. Virginia was not in favor of leaving the Union before the Civil War, but when President Lincoln called for volunteers to stop the secession movement, Virginia formed her own volunteer army, led by Robert E. Lee, and seceded from the Union. Many western counties opposed this decision and maintained a government loyal to the Union. In 1863 48 of these counties formed the state of West Virginia.

The majority of Civil War battles were fought on Virginia soil. Southern victories were achieved at the first and second battles of Bull Run (Manassas), during "Stonewall" Jackson's Valley Campaign, and at Fredericksburg and Chancellorsville. Richmond, the Confederate capital, was assaulted repeatedly by Union troops,

Yorktown was the site of a bloody Civil War battle in 1862. This print depicts the bombardment of Confederate troops by Union forces. The siege forced the Southern army to retreat and withdraw to Richmond.

55

The end of the Civil War: General Robert E. Lee surrenders to Ulysses S. Grant at Appomattox Court House, Virginia, on April 9, 1865.

and the Shenandoah Valley was hotly contested because it supplied food for Confederate armies. Ironclad warships fought for the first time at Hampton Roads, where the Union's *Monitor* and the *Merrimack* (renamed *Virginia* by the Confederate Navy) clashed in 1862. Like the Revolutionary War, the Civil War ended in Virginia, with Lee's surrender to General Ulysses S. Grant at Appomattox on April 9, 1865.

After the war, the ravaged state of Virginia began again, with nothing on which to rebuild her fortunes. Virginia was not readmitted to the Union until 1870, after five years of military occupation by federal forces and political domination by the Radical Republicans of the Reconstruction era. During the 1880s, the state began to develop some industrial and agricultural diversity with the establishment of cigarette factories, textile plants, and shipyards. But opportunities were few, and thousands of people left the state—a pattern that continued into the early 1900s.

Unlike most states, Virginia benefited from the Great Depression of the 1930s in the form of federal programs that created new jobs and helped stem the outgoing flow of population. Then World War II, which the United States entered in 1941, brought thousands of servicemen, shipbuilders, and government officials, especially into the area around Washington, D.C., and Norfolk. Many of these people settled in Virginia after the war ended in 1945.

Postwar improvements in Virginia included extensive highway construction and completion of the Chesapeake Bay Bridge–Tunnel linking the Norfolk area with the Eastern Shore. Industrial growth in the clothing, metals, and machinery fields strengthened Virginia's economy, and tourism became a $4 billion business. Virginia's scenic Skyline Drive, seashore resorts, historic sites, and other attractions draw visitors from all over the country. Virginia adopted a new state constitution in 1971. Concerned with social issues and reform, it called for high-quality education for all, environmental conservation, and consumer protection.

Virginia: Land of Presidents

George Washington, 1st president of the United States, known as "father of Our Country," was born in Wakefield.

The 3rd president of the United States, Thomas Jefferson, was born in Albermarle County.

James Madison, a native of Port Conway, was America's 4th president.

James Monroe, the 5th president, was born in Westmoreland County.

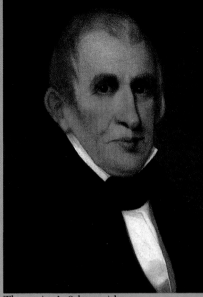

The nation's 9th president, William Henry Harrison, came from Berkeley.

John Tyler, a native of Greenway, was the 10th president.

America's 12th president, Zachary Taylor, was born in Orange County.

Woodrow Wilson, our nation's 28th president, was born in Staunton.

59

At right:
Cyrus McCormick, born near Lexington, Virginia, invented the first successful mechanical reaper in 1831 and revolutionized the agricultural industry.

Far right:
Confederate cavalry leader J.E.B. (Jeb) Stuart was born in Patrick County. After distinguishing himself in daring cavalry raids against Union forces, Stuart briefly took command of Stonewall Jackson's corps at Chancellorsville in 1863.

Education

Virginia had the first free schools in what is now the United States: the Syms Free School, founded at Hampton in 1634, and the Easton Free School in the same community, founded in 1640. Virginia's state-wide public school system began in 1870. The first institution of higher education in Virginia was the College of William and Mary. It was founded in 1693, and is the second oldest university in the United States. By the time Virginia entered the Union in 1788, two other colleges and universities had been established: what is now Washington and Lee University (1749) and Hampden-Sydney College (1776).

The People

Some 72 percent of Virginians live in metropolitan areas. Approximately 95 percent of them were born in the United States. The largest religious groups in the state are the southern Baptists and the Methodists. Other sizable denominations are the National Baptists, Roman Catholics, Presbyterians, and Episcopalians.

Famous People

Many famous people were born in the State of Virginia. Here are a few:

Arthur Ashe became the first black tennis player to win the U.S. Open men's singles title in 1968.

Russell Baker is a writer and columnist whose work can be found in the New York Times.

Arthur Ashe 1943-93, Richmond. Tennis champion

Pearl Bailey 1918-1990 Newport News. Stage, screen, and TV singer

Russell Baker b.1925, Loudoun County. Pulitzer Prize-winning humor columnist

Warren Beatty b.1937, Richmond. Actor and Academy Award-winning director: *Reds*

William Becknell 1796-1865, Amherst County. Blazer of the Santa Fe Trail

George Caleb Bingham 1811-1879, Augusta

County. Painter

Richard E. Byrd 1888-1957, Winchester. Antarctic explorer and first man to fly over the South Pole and the North Pole

June Carter b.1929, Maces Spring. Country and western singer

Willa Cather 1873-1947, Winchester. Pulitzer Prize-winning novelist: *One of Ours, A Lost Lady*

June Carter is the daughter of Mother Maybelle Carter of the country music group, the Original Carter Family. June married Johnny Cash in 1967.

Willa Cather's family moved from Virginia to Nebraska when she was nine. Her childhood there would inspire her writings about the western frontier.

George Rogers Clark 1752-1818, near Charlottesville. Revolutionary War general

Roy Clark b.1933, Meherrin. Country and western singer and musician

William Clark 1770-1838, Caroline County. Frontiersman and co-leader of the Lewis and Clark Expedition

Henry Clay 1777-1852, Hanover County. Senator and drafter of the Missouri Compromise

Patsy Cline 1932-1963, Winchester. Country and western singer.

Joseph Cotten b. 1905, Petersburg. Film actor:

Joseph Cotten was brought to Hollywood by Orson Welles to star in Citizen Kane *in 1941.*

Thomas Jefferson founded the University of Virginia in 1819, where he developed the design and architecture of the campus.

Citizen Kane

Ray Dandridge b. 1913, Richmond. Hall of Fame baseball player.

Jubal Early 1816-1894, Franklin County. Confederate army general

Ella Fitzgerald b.1918, Newport News. Jazz singer

Ellen Glasgow 1874-1945, Richmond. Pulitzer Prize-winning novelist: *This Is Our Life*

William Henry Harrison 1773-1841, Charles City County. Ninth President of the United States

Patrick Henry 1736-1799, Studley. Revolutionary War patriot and orator

Sam Houston 1793-1863, Lexington. Soldier and president of the Republic of Texas

Thomas Jefferson 1743-1826, Albemarle County. Third President of the United States

Joseph E. Johnston 1807-1891, near Farmville. Confederate Army general

Francis Parkinson Keyes 1885-1970, Charlottesville. Novelist: *Dinner at Antoine's*

Christopher Kraft b.1924, Phoebus. NASA flight director

Francis Lightfoot Lee 1734-1797, Westmoreland County. Politician and signer of the Declaration of Independence

Light-Horse Harry Lee 1756-1818, Prince William County. Revolutionary War cavalry officer

Richard Henry Lee 1732-1794, Stratford. Revolutionary War patriot and signer of the Declaration of Independence

Although he became Chief Justice of the Supreme Court, Marshall had little formal schooling as a boy and studied law only briefly.

Robert E. Lee 1807-1870, Stratford. Confederate Army general

Meriwether Lewis 1774-1809, Albemarle County. Co-leader of the Lewis and Clark Expedition

Shirley MacLaine b.1934, Richmond. Academy Award-winning actress: *Terms of Endearment*

James Madison 1751-1836, Port Conway. Fourth President of the United States

Moses Malone b.1954, Petersburg. Basketball

"Slammin' Sammy" Snead was thought to have one of the greatest natural swings in golf, winning more than 100 championships.

player

John Marshall 1755-1835, Germantown. Chief Justice of the Supreme Court

Cyrus McCormick 1809-1884, Rockbridge County. Inventor of the reaper

James Monroe 1758-1831, Westmoreland County. Fifth President of the United States

Wayne Newton b.1942, Norfolk. Pop singer

George Pickett 1825-1875, Richmond. Confederate Army general

Lewis F. Powell b.1907, Suffolk. Supreme Court justice

Chester Puller 1898-1971, West Point. World War II Marine Corps general

Jennings Randolph 1753-1813, Williamsburg. Attorney general and secretary of state

John Randolph 1773-1833, Prince George County. U.S. senator

Peyton Randolph 1721-1775, Williamsburg. First

Ralph Sampson was the first player chosen in the 1983 draft of college players.

president of the Continental Congress

Walter Reed 1851-1902, Glouster County. Discovered the cause of yellow fever

Bill Robinson 1878-1949, Richmond. Stage and screen tap dancer

Ralph Sampson b.1960, Harrisonburg. Basketball player.

George C. Scott b.1927, Wise. Academy Award-winning actor: *Patton*

Randolph Scott 1903-1987, Orange County. Western

film actor: *Ride the High Country*

Winfield Scott 1786-1866, Petersburg. Mexican War general

Kate Smith 1909-1986, Greenville. Ballad and pop singer

Sam Snead b.1912, Hot Springs. Professional golfer

Born a slave, Booker T. Washington moved to West Virginia with his family after the slaves were freed. There he started work at the age of nine, laboring in a salt furnace and a coal mine.

George Washington attended school until he was fifteen, after which he became a surveyor.

James Ewall Brown "Jeb" Stuart 1833-1864, Patrick County. Confederate cavalry commander

William Styron 1925-93, Newport News. Pulitzer Prize-winning novelist: *The Confessions of Nat Turner*

Fran Tarkenton b.1940, Richmond. Football quarterback

Lawrence Taylor b. 1959, Williamsburg. Football player.

Zachary Taylor 1784-1850, Orange County. Twelfth President of the United States

George Henry Thomas 1816-1870, Southampton County. Union Army general

Nat Turner 1800-1831, Southampton County. Leader of a slave revolt

John Tyler 1790-1862, Charles City County. Tenth President of the United States

S.S. Van Dine 1888-1939, Charlottesville. Mystery writer: *The Gracie Allen Murder Case*

Alexander Vandegrift 1887-1973, Charlottesville. World War II Marine Corps general

Booker T. Washington 1856-1915, Franklin County. Founder of Tuskegee Institute

George Washington 1732-1799, Westmoreland County. First President of the United States

Woodrow Wilson 1856-1924, Staunton. Twenty-

eighth President of the
United States
Tom Wolfe b.1931,
Richmond. Essayist and
novelist: *The Right Stuff*,
Bonfire of the Vanities

Colleges and Universities
There are many colleges
and universities in Virginia.
Here are the more
prominent, with their
locations, dates of founding,
and enrollments.

Bridgewater College,
Bridgewater 1880, 921
College of William and Mary,
Williamsburg, 1917, 7,732
Eastern Mennonite College,
Harrisonburg, 1917, 1,070
Emory and Henry College,
Emory, 1838, 780
George Mason University,
Fairfax, 1960, 20,829
Hampden-Sydney College,
Hampden-Sydney, 1776,
945
Hampton University, Hampton,
1868, 5,704
Hollins College, Hollins, 1842,
991

James Madison University,
Harrisonburg, 1908, 11,203
Longwood College, Farmville,
1884, 3,202
Lynchburg College, Lynchburg,
1903, 2,379
Mary Baldwin College,
Staunton, 1842, 800
Mary Washington College,
Fredericksburg, 1908, 3,432
Old Dominion University,
Norfolk, 1930, 16,561
Radford University, Radford,
1910, 9,432
Randolph-Macon College,
Ashland, 1830, 1,118
Roanoke College, Salem, 1842,
1,677
Saint Paul's College,
Lawrenceville, 1888, 750
Sweet Briar College,
Lynchburg, 1901, 600
University of Richmond,
Richmond, 1830, 4,579
University of Virginia,
Charlottesville, 1819, 17,604
*Virginia Commonwealth
University*, Richmond, 1838,
21,939
Virginia Military Institute,
Lexington, 1839, 1,265

*Virginia Polytechnic and State
University*, Blacksburg,
1872, 23,637
Virginia State University,
Petersburg, 1882, 4,435
Virginia Union University,
Richmond, 1865, 1,511
Virginia Wesleyan College,
Norfolk, 1961, 1,513
Washington & Lee University,
Lexington, 1749, 1,985

**Where To Get More
Information**
Virginia Chamber of
Commerce
9 South Fifth Street
Richmond, VA 23219
1-800-VISITVA

West Virginia

   The great seal of the state of West Virginia is circular. In the center is a drawing of a rock, symbolizing stability, with the date "June 20, 1863"—the date on which West Virginia became a state. To the left of the rock is a farmer with his right hand resting on the handle of a plow and an axe in his left hand. There is a sheaf of wheat and a cornstalk nearby. To the right of the rock is a miner with a pickaxe on his shoulder. To the far right are barrels and lumps of minerals, as well as an anvil with a sledge hammer on top of it. These represent the state's industries. Below the rock are two crossed hunter's rifles and the cap of liberty to indicate that West Virginia's freedom and liberty were won and will be protected. Around the circle is printed "State of West Virginia" as well as the state motto. The seal, adopted in 1863, was designed by Joseph H. Diss Debar.

WEST VIRGINIA

At a Glance

Capital: Charleston

State Flower: Rhododendron

Major Industries: Machinery, paper and wood products

Major Crops: Corn, beans, beets, hay, oats, cabbage

Size: 24,232 square miles (41st largest)
Population: 1,812,194 (35th largest)

State Bird: Cardinal

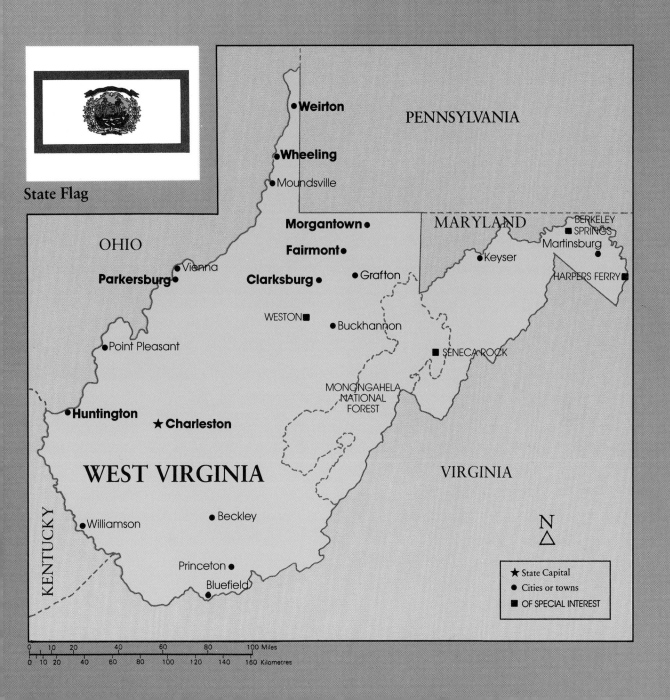

State Flag

PENNSYLVANIA

● **Weirton**

● **Wheeling**

● Moundsville

OHIO

Morgantown ●

Fairmont ●

● Vienna

Parkersburg ●

Clarksburg ●   ● Grafton

WESTON ■

● Buckhannon

● Point Pleasant

■ SENECA ROCK

MONONGAHELA
NATIONAL
FOREST

● **Huntington**

★ **Charleston**

WEST VIRGINIA

MARYLAND

BERKELEY
■ SPRINGS
Martinsburg
●

HARPERS FERRY ■

● Keyser

VIRGINIA

KENTUCKY

● Williamson

● Beckley

Princeton ●

Bluefield ●

N
△

| ★ State Capital |
| ● Cities or towns |
| ■ OF SPECIAL INTEREST |

0 10 20   40   60   80   100 Miles
0 10 20   40   60   80   100 120   140   160 Kilometres

State Flag

The flag of the state was adopted in 1929, after many other flags had been used. In the center, on a white background with a blue border, are the figures from the state seal. Below is the state motto and above is written "State of West Virginia." A wreath of rhododendrons is located to the left and the right of the figures.

State Motto

Montani Semper Liberi
The Latin motto is translated "Mountaineers Are Always Free," and it was adopted with the state seal in 1863.

Moats Falls, located on the Tygart River, is one of the many rapids in West Virginia, a state that prides itself on being the white-water capital of the east.

State Name and Nicknames

West Virginia was originally a part of Virginia, which was named after Elizabeth I of England—the "Virgin Queen." The counties that now make up the state split off from Virginia in 1861, after that state seceded from the Union.

The Allegheny Mountains located in West Virginia have given it the official nickname the *Mountain State* and the unofficial one of *Switzerland of America*. Because of its unusual shape, having two "panhandles," it has also been called the *Panhandle State*.

State Flower

The state flower is the rhododendron, *Rhododendron maximum*. Also called the big laurel, it was adopted by the state legislature in 1903 following a vote by school children. Other names for the flower are deer-laurel, cow-plant, rose bay, and spoon-hutch.

State Tree

Acer sacchaurm, the red maple, was selected the state tree in 1949. It was named following a vote by school children and civic clubs.

State Bird

The cardinal, *Richmondena cardinalis cardinalis*, was selected as the official bird in 1949.

State Capital

The first capital of the state was Wheeling. In 1870, Charleston was named, and in 1875 it was moved back to Wheeling. Charleston became the capital again in 1877 by popular vote. A

State Animal

Named in 1973, the black bear, *Euarctos americanus*, is the state animal.

State Fish

The brook trout, *Salvelinus fontinalis*, was adopted as state fish in 1973.

State Fruit

The apple was designated as state fruit in 1972.

Coal is one of West Virginia's most important resources.

State Songs

West Virginia has three state songs. The first was "This Is My West Virginia," by Mrs. Iris Bell. In 1947, "West Virginia, My Home Sweet Home" by Colonel Julian G. Hearne, was selected. In 1961 "The West Virginia Hills" with words by the Reverend David King and music by H. E. Engle was also chosen. King asked that his wife Ellen for whom he had written the words be credited with it.

Population

The population of West Virginia in 1992 was 1,812,194, making it the 35th most populous state. Approximately 99 percent of West Virginians were born in the United States, and many of their ancestors came from Germany, Great Britain, Hungary, Ireland, Italy, and Poland.

Seneca Rocks is one of many park areas and one of the most popular rock-climbing spots in the east.

Industries

The principal industries of the state are mining, mineral and chemical production, primary metals, timber, and stone, clay, and glass products. The chief products are machinery, plastic and hardwood products, fabricated metals, organic and inorganic chemicals, aluminum, and steel.

In addition, the unsurpassed beauty of West Virginia makes it a tourist attraction which earned $2.6 billion in 1992.

Agriculture

The chief crops of the state are apples, peaches, hay, tobacco, corn, wheat, oats, and barley. West Virginia is also a livestock state, and there are estimated to be some 520,000 cattle, 32,000 hogs and pigs, 76,000 sheep, and 1.2 million chickens on its farms. Oak, yellow poplar, hickory, walnut, and cherry trees are harvested for

timber, and crushed stone, sand and gravel, salt, cement, and dimension stone are important mineral resources.

Government

The governor is elected to a four-year term, as are the secretary of state, auditor, treasurer, attorney general, and commissioner of agriculture. The state legislature consists of a 34-member senate and a 100-member house of delegates. There are 17 senatorial districts in the state, each of which elects two senators, and the delegates are elected

West Virginia's lumber industry produces hardwoods for other states and for small furniture factories in-state.

West Virginia

Charleston serves as an industrial center, bringing together the resources of the Kanawha River valley.

either by county or by delegate districts, according to population. The most recent state constitution was adopted in 1872. In addition to its two senators, West Virginia has three representatives in the U.S. House of Representatives. The state has 5 votes in the electoral college.

Sports

The mountains and rivers of the state have made it popular with hunters and fishermen. White-water rafting has also become a popular sport.

Major Cities

Charleston (population 57,287). Settled in 1794, Charleston is the capital of the state and is the largest city in the state. Daniel Boone lived here until 1795. In 1789 he was appointed as lieutenant colonel on the county militia, and served in the Virginia assembly that year. As a salt center it became important in 1824. Charleston is the trade center for the Great Kanawha Valley. Here the coal, oil, natural gas, and brine make it one of the most important chemical and glass production centers in the country.

> *Places to visit in Charleston:* the State Capitol, the Governor's Mansion, the Cultural Center, the Sunrise Art Museum, the Sunrise Children's Museum, the Elk Rover Scenic Drive, Coonskin Park, and Kanawha State forest.

Huntington (population 54,844). Founded in 1871, Huntington was started by the millionaire president of the Chesapeake & Ohio Railroad, Collis P. Huntington. Commerce and industry have made it the most populous city in the state. Glass, railroad products, and metals are its most important industries.

> *Places to visit in Huntington:* the Huntington Museum of Art, Camden Park, and Heritage Village. There are

also tours through the Blenko Glass Company and the Pilgram Glass Corporation.

Wheeling (population 34,882). Settled in 1769 by Colonel Ebenezer Zane, it was the first settlement on the Ohio River. It is located on the site of Fort Henry—a fort built to protect settlers from Indians. It was the state capital from 1863 to 1870 and later from 1875 to 1885. In 1861 and 1862 the state constitution was framed in Wheeling. Due to its central location on the Ohio River, Wheeling served as an important stop for early travelers. Later Wheeling became an important resource for coal, oil, and natural gas.

Places to visit in Wheeling:
Oblebay Park; Fort Van Meter and Fort Henry (1774); and Monument Place, a mansion dating from 1789.

Places to Visit

The National Park Service maintains five areas in the state of West Virginia: Harpers Ferry National Historical Park, New River Gorge National River, part of the Chesapeake and Ohio Canal National Historical Park, part of the Appalachian National Scenic Trail, and the Monongahela National Forest. In addition, there are 34 state recreation areas.

Beckley: Beckley Exhibition Coal Mine. Visitors may tour the mine in coal cars.

Berkeley Springs: The Castle. This house, built in 1886, is patterned after Berkeley Castle in England.

Charles Town: Jefferson County Courthouse. Built in 1836, this was the site of the trial of John Brown.

Clarksburg: Stealey-Goff-Vance House. This restored home, built in 1807, exhibits collection of antique furniture, tools, and Indian artifacts.

Elkins: The Old Mill. This 1877 grist mill is still in use.

Harpers Ferry: Harpers Ferry National Historic Park. The old town has been restored to its appearance when

The Sternwheel Regatta Festival in Charleston is the largest of the state's festivals and includes concerts and other entertainment in addition to the regatta itself.

John Brown led his raid in 1859.

Hillsboro: Pearl S. Buck Birthplace Museum. The birthplace of the Nobel Prize-winning author has been restored to its appearance in 1892.

Martinsburg: General Adam Stephen House. Built from 1774 to 1789, this is the restored home of Adam Stephen, a Revolutionary War general and surgeon.

Philippi: Covered Bridge. Built in 1852, it is the only two-laned bridge of its type in daily use on a federal highway.

Events

There are many events and organizations that schedule activities of various kinds in the state of West Virginia. Here are some of them.

Sports: Sternwheel Regatta Festival (Charleston), horse racing at Charles Town Turf Club (Charles Town), Tucker County Alpine Winter Festival (Davis), Tri-State Fair and Regatta (Huntington), Mountaineer Balloon Festival (Morgantown), Horse Show (Shepherdstown), horse racing (Weirton).

Arts and Crafts: Appalachian Arts and Crafts Festival (Beckley), Apple Butter Festival (Berkeley Springs), Rhododendron Outdoor Arts and Crafts Festival (Charleston), Augusta Heritage Arts Festival (Elkins), Mountain Heritage Arts and Crafts Festival (Harpers Ferry), Harvest Moon Festival (Parkersburg), Mountaineer State Art and Craft Fair (Ripley), Stonewall Jackson Heritage Arts and Crafts Jubilee (Weirton).

Music: West Virginia Jazz Festival (Charleston), Jamboree in the Hills (Wheeling), Wheeling Symphony (Wheeling).

Entertainment: West Virginia Strawberry Festival (Buckhannon), Vandalia Gathering (Charleston), Jefferson County Fair (Charles Town), West Virginia Italian Heritage Festival (Clarksburg), Mountain State Forest Festival (Elkins), Three Rivers Coal Festival (Fairmont), Treasure Mountain Festival (Franklin), Taylor County Fair (Grafton), Election Day 1860 (Harpers Ferry), Old Tyme Christmas (Harpers Ferry), State Fair (Lewisburg), Pioneer Days (Marlinton), Hardy County Heritage Weekend (Moorfield), Parkersburg Homecoming (Parkersburg), West Virginia Honey Festival (Parkersburg), Barbour County Fair (Philippi), Mason County Fair (Point Pleasant), West Virginia Black Walnut Festival (Ripley), Nicholas County Fair (Summersville), Oglebayfest (Wheeling), Festival of Lights (Wheeling), King Coal Festival (Williamson).

Tours: House and Garden Tour (Charles Town).

Theater: Theatre West Virginia (Beckley), Hatfields and McCoys (Beckley), The Actors Guild Playhouse (Parkersburg).

The Land and the Climate

West Virginia is bordered on the west by Kentucky and Ohio; on the north by Ohio, Pennyslvania, and Maryland; on the east by Maryland and Virginia; and on the south by Virginia. The state has three main land regions: the Appalachian Ridge and Valley Region, the Appalachian Plateau, and the Blue Ridge.

The Appalachian Ridge and Valley Region covers a wide strip along the eastern border of West Virginia. The Allegheny Mountains, part of the Appalachian system, are located here. Their peaks alternate with valleys where swift streams make their way through the sedimentary rock that underlies the region. Caves are common, and the mountainsides are forested. Hogs, poultry, sheep, and dairy and beef cattle are raised in the area, which also has coal mines and sand and gravel quarries.

The Allegheny Highlands, in eastern West Virginia, have thick forests, beautiful peaks, and fertile valleys.

The Cumberland Mountain region lies west of the Allegheny Highlands. This scenic area includes forested hills, tablelands, and streams.

The Appalachian Plateau covers most of the state west of the Appalachian Ridge and Valley Region. This is rugged country with narrow valleys, flat-topped uplands, and rounded hills. Many mountains in the northwestern section are more than 4,000 feet above sea level. Most of the state's coal, salt, oil, and natural gas deposits are located here. It is also a region of dairy and beef-cattle farms, fruit and vegetable crops, and vineyards.

West Virginia is known for its wealth of natural resources. The unspoiled beauty of the state's national parks and recreation areas attracts a large number of tourists, including many fishermen and white-

water rafters. Historically, West Virginia's coal mines were integral to the industrial development of the country. The state also has rich deposits of natural gas, oil, salt, and timber; these resources support thriving glass, chemical, and metal industries.

Much of West Virginia is mountainous, and its rugged hills contain many mineral resources.

The Blue Ridge Mountains touch West Virginia at the tip of the Eastern Panhandle. Their slopes and valleys support apple and peach orchards on fertile soil overlying the igneous (fire-formed) rock that occurs in this part of the Appalachian system.

Summer temperatures in West Virginia average 74 degrees Fahrenheit in the valley regions; 68 degrees F. is the norm for the mountains. In January, temperatures rarely fall below 29 degrees F. in the mountains and are slightly higher in the valleys. Rainfall averages 44 inches yearly, with snowfall varying from 20 to 35 inches throughout the state.

The History

The first residents of what would become West Virginia were the ancient mound builders—the Adena people of 2,000 to 3,000 years ago and their successors, the Hopewell, of 1,500 to 2,000 years ago. They constructed great mounds of earth that were ceremonial sites and smaller mounds in which they buried their dead. They practiced agriculture, knew how to make pottery, and carved useful and ritual objects from soft stone. Many of their earthworks can still be seen at Moundsville, in the Northern Panhandle, and in the Great Kanawha Valley. Excavations have uncovered elaborately adorned human skeletons and artifacts of great beauty.

When European explorers arrived in the 1670s, the mound builders had long since vanished, and the area was a hunting ground for several Indian tribes from the north and east. The Cherokee, Conoy, Delaware, Shawnee, and Susquehanna came into the mountainous region to hunt during the summer and gathered salt from pools of brine.

Present-day West Virginia was part of the territory granted to the London Company by King James I of England for the Virginia colony in 1606. Its remoteness discouraged settlement, and the first non-Indian to visit the region was probably the German explorer John Lederer and his companions, who reached the Blue Ridge in 1669. Two years later, Thomas Batts and Robert Fallam came into the region in search of furs and transportation routes.

Morgan ap Morgan of Delaware, who moved into the Bunker Hill section of the Eastern Panhandle in 1726, is credited with being the first permanent colonial settler. Others soon followed, many of them Germans from Pennsylvania, who established a settlement called New Mecklenburg (now Shepherdstown) in 1727. Other newcomers were Welsh and Scots-Irish farmers who settled in the Eastern Panhandle, the Ohio Valley, and along the Greenbrier and New Rivers.

The Indians resisted this movement into their territory by raiding settlements. To defend themselves, the pioneers built forts and blockhouses, some of which grew into towns and cities. Among them were Forts Henry (now Wheeling), Lee (now Charleston), and Randolph (now Point Pleasant). During the French and Indian Wars, the British fought the French and their Indian allies for control of the region. In 1754 George Washington led an unsuccessful raid against the French in what is now West Virginia, and the following year the French and Indians defeated British general Edward Braddock in a number of battles.

Coal was discovered in 1742 and would eventually become a major source of revenue for the state, but only after railroads began expanding in the mid-1800s. Lumber became important after 1755, with the advent of water-powered sawmills.

King George III refused, in 1763, to let the colonists settle on land west of the Alleghenies until treaties could be made with the Indians, but many Virginia pioneers ignored these orders and moved west. In 1768 treaties were signed with the Cherokee and the Iroquoian-speaking Mingo, and by 1775, some 30,000 settlers were living between the Allegheny Mountains and the Ohio River. These people were far from the seat of Virginia government at Williamsburg, and they began to demand their own government as early as 1776. Meanwhile, George Washington's brother, Charles, had laid out the city of Charles Town, which was named for him, in 1768. The town of Bath, a health resort at Berkeley Springs, had been established two years earlier.

The western settlers sent many men to fight in the Revolutionary War. Indian armies led by British officers invaded the area three times between 1777 and 1782, but they were repulsed. Industry began to develop even during the Revolution, and after the war ended in 1783, the first iron furnace west of the Alleghenies was built in the Northern Panhandle. In 1808 the Kanawha Valley began producing large quantities of salt, and the nation's first natural gas well was discovered at Charleston in 1815.

James Wilson accidentally discovered the nation's first natural gas well at Charleston in 1815. The discovery offered a major opportunity for West Virginia's economy to expand and prosper.

Harper's Ferry (then in Virginia) was the site of John Brown's unsuccessful 1859 raid on the federal arsenal there.

During the early 1800s, western settlers felt increasingly estranged from eastern Virginians. The easterners owned large plantations and used the Atlantic Ocean for commerce. The westerners were primarily small farmers who carried out trade on the waterways flowing toward the Mississippi River. They felt that their interests were ignored by the state government, and bitter disputes broke out over slavery, taxation, education, and other issues. A crisis became imminent in 1859 when abolitionist John Brown and his followers seized the federal arsenal at Harpers Ferry. This attempt to incite a slave uprising was a prelude to the Civil War, and resulted in Brown's execution in Charleston.

Abolitionist John Brown was convinced that direct military action was the only means by which slavery could be eliminated from the United States. He led violent anti-slavery factions in Kansas during the 1850s and was captured by Robert E. Lee after his raid at Harper's Ferry. Brown was hanged for treason on December 2, 1859.

A view of Wheeling in 1854. The city was an important commercial and political center during the Civil War era and was designated the state capital in 1863.

The Civil War made West Virginia a state. After the Common-wealth of Virginia left the Union in April 1861, representatives of the western counties, which had opposed secession, held a series of meetings. In the Second Wheeling Convention, these representatives adopted a Declaration of Rights that branded the secession ordinance

illegal and reorganized state government as the Restored Government of Virginia. That August the western counties approved the formation of a new state, originally named Kanawha. The name was later changed to West Virginia, which was admitted as the 35th state in 1863, with its capital at Wheeling.

However, West Virginia was not without Confederate sympathizers, two of whom would play dramatic roles in the Civil War: General Thomas J. "Stonewall" Jackson and Belle Boyd, the renowned Confederate spy. Some 8,000 West Virginians fought for the South, while 30,000 joined Union forces. Extended conflict occurred at Philippi in April 1861, in a clash for control of the Baltimore and Ohio Railroad. Throughout the year and into 1862, federal forces under Generals George McClellan and William S. Rosecrans drove Confederate raiders back into Virginia. The town of Romney changed hands 56 times during the course of the war.

Virginia asked West Virginia to reunite with it after the war ended, but West Virginia refused. The war had left West Virginia a new state, but one in turmoil. Ruined property, heavy debt, and residual bitterness hampered recovery. Returning Confederate veterans were denied the vote until 1871.

The development of railroads allowed West Virginia to exploit valuable mineral and timber resources, and coal mining became a major industry. But working conditions in the mines were very bad: a single explosion in 1907 killed 361 miners. The first miners' strike for better wages and conditions was organized by the United Mine Workers in 1912. Twelve miners were killed in battles with mine guards, and the state militia had to intervene. In 1913 Governor Henry D. Hatfield proposed a guaranteed nine-hour work day and the right to organize unions, and peace was restored for a time.

World War I was a boom time for West Virginia. Its raw materials and manufactured products were essential to the war effort. But trouble in the coal fields flared up again after the war. In 1920 mine owners at Matewan locked union miners out of their jobs. Miners were evicted from their company-owned homes. Riots occurred, and 500 federal soldiers were sent in. The governor declared martial law, and armed conflict over the right to organize continued in 1921. The state indicted 543 miners for taking part in a four-day battle near Blair, and 22 of them were tried for treason against the state. Despite their acquittal, most miners left the union and many left the state.

Thomas J. "Stonewall" Jackson was born in Clarksburg when it was still part of Virginia. He secured an appointment to the U.S. Military Academy in 1842. When the Civil War broke out, Jackson joined the Confederate army and became one of its most honored military leaders.

During the Great Depression of the 1930s, the National Recovery Administration effected improvements by which mine owners shortened hours, raised wages, and improved working conditions, and the mining industry rallied. During World War II, mines and factories were humming with activity, as they turned out materials for the armed forces. The first synthetic rubber plant was established near Charleston in 1943.

After the war, the federal government took over many of the mines after a series of work stoppages. A decreased demand for coal, and automation in the mines during the 1950s, created widespread unemployment in West Virginia, and many miners left the state in search of other jobs. But the chemical and synthetic-textile industries, which used the state's coal, oil, salt, and water resources, were on the upswing. The glass and metal industries prospered. West Virginia continues to work to diversify its economy and use its resources, including natural gas, petroleum, building stone, and timber.
Many visitors believe that its natural beauty is unsurpassed in the East, and tourism brings in well over $1 billion per year.

Education

Pioneer children in western Virginia attended school in log cabins that also served as churches. West Virginia established a free school system in 1863, after it joined the Union. The first institutions of higher education in the region were Marshall University and West Liberty State College, both founded in 1837. Bethany College was established in 1840, and West Virginia University in 1867.

Charleston is the capital of West Virginia and its largest city. The state's chemical industry, an important component of its economy, is centered here.

Famous People

Many famous people were born in the state of West Virginia. Here are a few:

Newton Baker 1871-1937, Martinsburg. Public official and Secretary of War.

George Brett b.1953, Moundsville. Baseball player

Pearl S. Buck 1892-1973, Hillsboro. Nobel Prize-winning novelist: *The Good Earth*

Thomas Jonathan "Stonewall" Jackson 1824-1863, Clarksburg (then Virginia). Confederate general

Don Knotts b.1924, Morgantown. Film and TV comedian

John Knowles b.1926, Fairmont. Novelist: *A Separate Peace*

Bill Mazeroski b. 1936, Wheeling. Baseball player and hero of 1960 World Series.

John McKay b.1923, Everettsville. College and professional football coach

Walter Reuther 1907-1970, Wheeling. Labor leader

George C. Scott b. 1927, Wise. Actor

Harry F. Sinclair 1876-1956, Wheeling. Founder of oil company

Cyrus Vance b.1917, Clarksburg. Secretary of State under Carter

Teddy Weatherford 1903-1945, Bluefield. Jazz pianist

Jerry West b.1938, Chelyan. Basketball player

Colleges and Universities

There are many colleges and universities in West Virginia. Here are the more prominent, with their locations, dates of founding, and enrollment.

Alderson-Broaddus College, Philippi, 1871, 812

Bethany College, Bethany, 1840, 761

Bluefield State College, Bluefield, 1895, 2,931

Concord College, Athens, 1872, 2,960

Davis and Elkins College, Elkins, 1903, 922

Fairmont State College, Fairmont, 1867, 6,615

Glenville State College, Glenville, 1872, 2,358

Marshall University, Huntington, 1837, 12,744

Salem-Teikyo University, Salem, 1888, 715

Shepherd College, Shepherdstown, 1871, 3,559

West Liberty State College, West Liberty, 1837, 2,377

West Virginia Institute of Technology, Montgomery, 1895, 3,051

West Virginia State College, Institute, 1891, 4,896

West Virginia University, Morgantown, 1867, 22,712

West Virginia Wesleyan College, Buckhannon, 1890, 1,655

Wheeling College, Wheeling, 1954, 1,438

Where To Get More Information

Travel West Virginia
Department of Commerce
State Capitol Complex
Charleston, WV 25305
1-800-CALLWVA

Further Reading

Aylesworth, Thomas G. and Virginia L. *Let's Discover the States: Atlantic.* New York: Chelsea House, 1988.

District of Columbia

Duffield, Judy, and others. *Washington, D.C.: The Complete Guide.* New York: Random House, 1982.

Fradin, Dennis B. *From Sea to Shining Sea: Washington.* Chicago: Childrens Press, 1992.

Fronek, Thomas, ed. *The City of Washington: An Illustrated History.* New York: Alfred A. Knopf, 1977.

Kent, Deborah. *America the Beautiful: Washington, D.C.* Chicago: Childrens Press, 1991.

Virginia

Campbell, Elizabeth A. *Jamestown: the Beginning.* Boston: Little, Brown, 1974.

Dabney, Virginius. *Virginia: The New Dominion.* New York: Doubleday, 1971.

Fradin, Dennis B. *From Sea to Shining Sea: Virginia.* Chicago: Childrens Press, 1992.

McNair, Sylvia. *America the Beautiful: Virginia.* Chicago: Childrens Press, 1989.

Rubin, Louis D., Jr. *Virginia: A Bicentennial History.* New York: W.W. Norton, 1977.

West Virginia

Bailey, Bernadine. *Picture Book of West Virginia*, rev. ed. Niles: Whitman, 1980.

Carpenter, Allan. *West Virginia*, rev. ed. Chicago: Children's Press, 1979.

Fradin, Dennis B. *West Virginia in Words and Pictures.* Chicago: Children's Press, 1980.

Stein, R. Conrad. *America the Beautiful: West Virginia.* Chicago: Childrens Press, 1991.

Williams, John A. *West Virginia: A Bicentennial History.* New York: W.W. Norton, 1976.

Numbers in italics refer to illustrations

Photo Credits